BASIC
LIFE
SKILLS
POETRY

METS Poetry Club
Jersey City N.J.

James Curtis Geist

Editor

Dedicated to

Superintendent Damion Frye,

the Staff and Teachers,

the NJEA Leadership

and the students of

METS Charter School

"Breathe in experience. Breathe out poetry."
                              -Muriel Rukeyser

"How can I know what I think till I see what I
    say."   -E.M. Forster

"If I waited for perfection...I would never write a
    word."   -Margaret Atwood

"Poetry is when an emotion has found a thought,
    and the thought has found words."
                              -Robert Frost

"In my life, I have never been free. I have never
    been able to do anything with freedom, except
    in the field of my writing."
                              -Langston Hughes

"Better to write for yourself and have no public,
    than to write for the public and have no self."
                              -Cyril Connolly

<u>Guns & Butter, Bread & Roses</u>
Poetry & Anecdotes *(July 2018)*

<u>Stories of the Heilige, Polter & Zeitgeist</u>
Poetry & Anecdotes *(January 2019)*

<u>The Presidents [1-45]</u>
(February 2019)

<u>Essential Geist: Volume I & II</u>
Poetry & Anecdotes *(February 2019)*

<u>Ragbag</u>
Poetry & Anecdotes *(March 2019)*

<u>My Canterbury Tale</u>
Poetry & Anecdotes *(March 2019)*

<u>Confession: Musings of Mischief</u>
Poetry & Anecdotes *(April 2019)*

**<u>Global History I, II, III & IV Notes
for Teachers</u>** *(May 2019)*

<u>Jimmy's Fishing Trip</u>
A Children's Book *(May 2019)*

**<u>United States History Notes for
Teachers</u>** *(June 2019)*

<u>Jimmy's Circus Trip</u>
A Children's Book *(May 2019)*

<u>Moonquakes</u>
Poetry & Anecdotes *(February 2020)*

TABLE OF CONTENTS

Contemplation

The roadway of life
is always bumpy
and never flows.

Sometimes it's dark,
sometimes it's light
But for me it's never bright.
Death may be an option
but I don't know if I want it.

I love my family and my friends here,
all I have left if room for tears.
I don't do it;
I know I would hurt them,
but I think I would be okay then.

It might be painful
but I won't be hurting,
I want to see colors
I want the world to be pastel –
maybe then I will not be in sad→full.

Mia Gonzalez
8th Grade

Phases

Love,
pain,
connection and
loss.
Growing mentally,
not always
physically.

Age;
not just
a number,
but
a menace.

Finally
Paradise.

Nevia Welch
8th Grade

Be Positive

sometimes life is tricky
sometimes thing go wrong
sometimes you feel out of place
sometimes you feel like you don't belong
sometimes bad things happen
sometimes you will feel scared
sometimes you need to focus on the
               positive
seek them and they will be there
step out of the darkness
and look into the light
the awful things won't vanish
but don't let them consume you
or it will make you miserable
and intensify your gloom
focus on your blessing
and let them shine
don't let the negative
be what defines you

Sophia Rosette
11th Grade

<u>Classical Conditioning</u>

When you sprout you adjust to your surroundings.
Relationships are among those daily life findings.
From toddlers to teens we learn every day,
From nurturing parents who guide us
on what and what not to say.
We respect society and
manners every day.

Life advances in our inherited path.
We're adults now and our offspring
have entered the draft.
It's now their turn to learn
as we pass what our parents taught us.
We connect with them and teach them
to daily build the trust.

The chain continues when
the grandchildren follow the path.
Soon the grand kids will enlist in
the lifelong learning draft.
It feels like an end,
but is a beginning.
We sprout and learn from
classical conditioning.

Shawn Bellemy
11th Grade

Moving On

I am not
selling a house,
I'm leaving a home.

Happy times together,
months spent alone.

Morning sickness,
baby loss,
labor and birth,
planting
my seeds
in
good strength.

Jocelyn Mendez
11th Grade

Running

This life was yours from the beginning,
this body was your creation,
every breath belongs to you.
Yet I have never stopped to thank you.

In this fast paced life,
I am run miles continuously,
out of breath I ask and take,
wanting more each time.

You give without complaint or hesitant eye,
I take all and leave temporarily,
just to come back for more and repeat.
Yet I have never stopped to thank you.

When will I stop running, I don't know.
When will I stop asking, I don't know.
When will I stop taking, I don't know.
But I will start thanking for the
things you have given and taken.

Naomi Alves
11th Grade

Precious

Life is precious.

150,000 people daily

are not guaranteed it.

Every second makes an impact in life,

every day you live consider yourself lucky.

Pray you live for another day,

Use your time wisely while you are here.

Abdul Elola
11th Grade

You only get
to live once,
but
if you
do it right,
once
is enough.

-*Mae West*

Is

Life
is not life
without
desire.

There are
many things
you cannot
get.

You can
have fun
or be tired,
but
you can
never forget.

Alexander Cepeda Santos
11th Grade

Roller Coaster

When I think of life,
people coming and going,
some living and some dying.

Life is a crazy roller coaster never knowing which
turn, twist or hill will be next.

Life comes in waves and when the cross currents
hit, you know how to face them.

Life will never be easy; anything in life worth
having is not easy.

The good waves are the best.
You will always be happy following your bliss.

Enjoy the ride.

Chelsea Diggs
11th Grade

Heart

Today was the absolute worst day ever.

Don't convince me there is good in everything,

when you take a closer look,

the world is an evil place.

Even if some goodness

does shine through once in a while,

satisfaction and happiness don't last.

It's not all true that

it's all in the mind and heart.

Bryan Diaz
11ᵗʰ Grade

Possibility

Without wings,
birds could only walk.
Without legs,
humans could only crawl.

We use whatever
was granted to us,
never diverging,
always creating as
we make our own path
and walk upon
our achievements.

We have been
given brains,
all is possible.
Nothing humans have
ever put its mind to
has failed to
become reality.

Ahmed Amashad
12th Grade

Other Happiness

How can I be happy?
Does money buy happiness?
I don't need to be rich,
I don't need to be popular,
I don't need a dozen cars.

I need a person
to make me feel safe,
who fights for me,
who really loves me,
one who makes me laugh.

The one thing I would
not want to change
for anything in the world
is I need to be happy
and that you be happy.

Marylacey Nunez
8th Grade

Searching

Some people cannot find happiness.

You cannot buy happiness.

You cannot be given happiness.

You cannot buy happiness.

Happiness is in all of us.

You have to look deep down

Inside yourself.

You'll find it.

Robert Johnson
8th Grade

Happiness

happiness isn't materialistic,
it isn't something to buy .
happiness is free,
free for everyone.
you just need to look
in the right place.
happiness is around you, me.
happiness can even be
found in sorrow,
if looking for it.
you are the key
to your happiness.

Anonymous
11th Grade

Most folks
are as happy
as they
make up
their minds
to be.

-Abraham Lincoln

Peace

Finding
happiness is
key.

It can
heal your
soul.

Once you
obtain inner
peace,

it will
make you feel
complete and
whole.

Yiannis Kourasis
11th Grade

Earned

Happiness can be you,
it can be me,
or it can be.

Everyone I see, travels around
like you and me.
It does not stay in one place,
for that would mean we all have to race.
It is happiness we all deserve,
for it is what we have earned.

There are many reasons
to feel the way you do,
 but I want to say this from me to you;
YOU are your own happiness.
Don't let anyone take it away.
For you day should be any
but a rainy day.

Synthia Horne
11th Grade

Conflicted

I don't know if I have it sometimes.

I don't know if I feel it sometimes.

Achievements
Friends

I grow weary about them sometimes.

What do I want to do with my life?

I don't believe I know it sometimes.

Do I really want the money
or
do I just want a good old time?

Natalya Gonzalez
12th Grade

Connection to Self

She was tired of running
From everything that haunted her

She was tired of searching
For a piece missing inside her

She wanted to be free to
Walk and smell the roses

She wanted to be happy
She decided to be
And so she was

Maricar Labasa
12th Grade

Love Yourself

You must love yourself before you can love others.
Don't indulge in self-loathing: it keeps you docile.
Curiosity in adventure is human, so take a chance
    in life.
Maintain a healthy lifestyle for a healthy mind.
Build bonds with friends, family and loved ones.

The key to happiness lies within you.
You must be true to yourself before you add
    others.
Don't be lazy, go outside, put on your shoes.
Find your adventure, a whole life to discover.

Train your body to train your mind.
Love your family, friends and others.
You have only one life;
the key to happiness lies within you.

Alexis Sanvicente
12th Grade

No Faking

Life is
what you
make it.
Fake it
until you
make it.
Happiness
you cannot
fake,
it will
just make
you sad.

Farah Elmassry
12th Grade

Breathing

As I lay here on my back
He places down papers in a stack.
He whispers *'breathe now child, breathe'*
And turns his back so he can leave.

The ink on the papers lay heavy and black.
The words certainly a lot to unpack.
Still, it does not take much to achieve
And so I try to breathe.

The time someone new comes back,
And he places a book atop the stack,
He says *'breathe now child, breathe.'*
And turns his back so he can leave.

The new pages smell like lilac
And the book makes my back crack.
Every time my chest heaves,
And still I try to breathe.

Again, someone else comes back.
And she adds a brick to the stack.
She projects, *'Breathe now child breathe!'*
As air grows tight, I grit my teeth.
And yet I try to breathe.

The brick is making my breathing lack
And I feel like I's having a panic attack.
Air grows tight, I grit my teeth,
And yet I try to breathe.

Now, all three people were back,
And each balanced their boulders on the stack,
The shout 'BREATHE NOW CHILD, BEATHE!'
And for once they did not leave.

When it comes to breathing, I starting to slack,
And I struggle to sit up with my aching back.
I'm starting to go numb from head to feet,
And this time, I cannot breathe.

Maya Josephine Kelly
11th Grade

You know
you are in love
when you can't
fall asleep because
reality if finally
better than your
dreams.

-Dr. Seuss

Flower

Today
I feel
like a
flower
blooming.

I close
the shades,
put some
water in,
let it sit.

On day three
when my hands
are clean,
I wake
and smile at
the sunshine
again.

Aaliyah Clark
6th Grade

What's Wrong?

What is going on?
Why are people looking at me?
Why is my heart beating so fast?

I don't like this feeling.
I feel scared though
nothing is going on.

What is happening?
I feel like I am running a race,
even though I am standing still.

Why are they looking at me?
Why can't I talk?
I feel like my mouth is shut closed.
What's wrong with me?

Lucas Rodriguez
11th Grade

Darkness

Darkness looms over his mind,
he wants her to leave it all behind.
The tears on his cheeks never dry,
every day he lets out a loud cry.

His mental state is parlous.
Without help, it will turn disastrous.
He longs for a friend or two,
so that way, him mind won't be so blue.

A bright light shines through, support
comes so he bids his dark thought adieu.
The boy smiles and is content.

His mental state rarely
goes back to being hellbent.

Ashley Rosa
12th Grade

Self-Care

To care for one's self is life,
that one does no matter the strife.
Sometimes life can get you down, and
you have no choice but to frown.

Sometimes a break is all you need,
to kickstart your day with a gleam.
Forget about your work,
 relax, play and rest until
the dark clouds go away.

Don't ignore your body, listen to its call.
Your body reminds you of a better cause.
Eat till your full, drink your limit,
keep going until your health is sufficient.

Whenever your mood starts feeling low,
go see a friend and say "Hello!"

Gabriel Elyazi
11th Grade

Tell Me You Love Me

Tell me you love me
Tell me it's not really over
Tell me we didn't just say goodbye
Tell me we can begin again
Tell me I am worth one last try.

Tell me you miss me
Tell me you think of me when you wake
Tell me I fill your dreams at night
Tell me this is all a mistake

Tell me you need me
Tell me you love me
Tell me I have a place in your life
Just tell me something

Makayla Thompson
6th Grade

You & Me

The sun is up
The sky is blue
Today is beautiful
and so are you.

Just me and you,
just us two
My lover; my friend
together with you
until the end

Through
good and bad
happy and sad
you and me

Zayna Rivera
6th Grade

Blinds

The way you glow through my blinds in the
morning, it makes me feel like you missed me.

Kissing my forehead to help me out of bed,
Making me rub the sleepy out of my eyes.

Are you asking me to come out and play?
Are you trusting me to wish away a rainy day?

I look above, the sky is blue.
It's a secret, but I trust you.

> If it wasn't for you,
> I could sleep forever.

> I am not mad,
> I just want breakfast.

Rahmir Jackson
11th Grade

Love-Hate Relationship

Sometimes we all need an escape
from all the commotion
Take a step back and look at the shape,
try not to give in to wild emotion.

The dreaded monster that consumes time
and entertains us
can feel like a crime,
when I lose my life, I am filled with disgust.

I enjoy the time we spend together,
my love is as light as a feather.
My love is as heavy as a wrecking ball
when it hits me in the face like a cannon ball.

We have a love-hate relationship.
Our story together is an encyclopedia.
At the end of the day,
I will never stop loving
my social media.

Sandrew Singh
12th Grade

Dishonesty

Think about life when you walk the streets,
the less petty people is better.
I look back and talk through a heartbeat,
everything is explained in the letter.

Going through stages in life,
high school, the single years,
how much of this time was cruel?
Look back at childhood gone.

I never knew life could be so cruel.
It shocked me when my best friend betrayed me.
I thought our relationship was a garden, a jewel,
she held me down, but now - freedom.

Your love and support is all I need.
Our friendship was extreme,
especially your dishonesty.
Never would I think you were so conceited,
I always did my part as I promised.

Nourhan Fathy
12th Grade

Best Friends

They will always
be there for you.
They will help you
with your problems too.

They will always
be right there.
True friends never
leave and disappear.

They will give you
joy and happiness.
You can have lots of friends
starting today.

Elijah Forde
12th Grade

Hidden Beauty

Natural beauty today tends to be dissembled,
Hidden threw a mask being undetected.
She fears people who are judgmental,
when they only saw a false perspective.

She continues to hide it underneath,
being unable to evince her fear,
she lives a never ending story of defect
that wants fixed but never makes it clear.

She applies makeup looking in the mirror,
feeling unsatisfied with work done,
continues to cry with a distant shimmer
saying never good enough.

She lives in the shadows wishing
her beauty could be displayed,
she never understood she
kept it under a mask gone astray.

Daniel Guzman
12th Grade

Curls on a Mission

I look in the mirror and do I see,
a curly headed young person looking at me.
Long and curly is a lie,
shrinkage brings it way up high.

You stare at the complexity of my hair
Why do you judge the texture of my curls?
It is radiant hair no matter the girl.

My locks suffered in the heat,
time after time being put on the beat.
I like the way my strands twist and stay light,
rebelling against society's demand
to lay straight without a fight.

I stand tall with my luscious locks,
society made me strong as a rock.
Stereotypes did not get the best of me,
I am who I am because of me.

Monserrat Noboa
12th Grade

Breaking

When I said
I love you,
it was all true.
When you
broke my heart,
I did not know
what to do.

At the end of the day,
I came back to you.
You were the
only one I knew.
Look
how much
I have grown,
not crying
over you.

Anonymous

Heartbreak

Jessica
is the name
of the girl
I want back.
Whenever I see her
my breathing becomes
an asthma attack.
Whenever we spend
time together, I am
always taken aback.
It is her care and attention
I love and lack.
I feel without her, my soul
and heart would turn black,
I wish this vixen would
cut me some slack.
She looked at me one day
and said, "Greg you are wack!"
I still can't stop thinking
of Jessica as "my snack."
I think her affections now
are aiming for Zach.
Better him than
my best mate Jack.

Gregory Proano
11th Grade

Colors of Rain

Twilight and evening bell
after the dark!
May there be no sadness of farewell
when I embark.

When you died that day,
my life was painted with gray,
in shades of self-blame,
suicide turns day into colors of dark rain forever,
colors in shame.

Life asked Death
"Why do people love me but hate you?"
Death responded,
"Because you are a beautiful lie
and I am the truth."

Ashely Perez
6th Grade

The Hard Work

There is a grieving process
when dealing with loss.
If you don't do
your grieving work
one can stay in
a state of depress.

You do not live
when grief is your life,
Sometimes losing someone
is for the better.
Losing someone you love is hard,
do your grieving work and
one day you get
back on track.

Anthony Guzman
8th Grade

I do not fear death.
I had been dead
billions and billions
of years
before I was born, and
had not suffered
the slightest
inconvenience
from it.

-Mark Twain

Energy Never Destroyed

Death can take years,
Death can take hours,
the sure thing is death will come.

As painful as it can be,
your day will come.
Remember,
energy can never be destroyed,
the soul will live on
and the body will die.

Life is planted,
Life is taken away,
live while you are alive
the sure thing is
everyone will die.

Ashlee Stevens
8th Grade

Grief

Sometimes
it takes a minute
to find
a special person,
a whole hour
to appreciate them,
just a day
to love them
and
an entire life
to
forget them.

Risaydelis Reyes
8th Grade

That Day

On that day
my soul
grew sick.
On that day
the day
went quick.
All my life
I will
miss you.
I promise
to
never
forget
you.

Synthia Horne
11th Grade

Lost

Death is near, that I know,
whispering to me, at my lowest.
"There is nothing to fear." he said,
"Your death will be peaceful" she said.

My death is anything but peaceful.
Do not wish to die.
Do not wish to disappear,
so much to live for.

Death has come to claim me.
Begged for mercy,
begged to live,
now I am nothing
but a lost soul.

Leslie Ramirez
11th Grade

Why?

Oh death, what a terrible thing,
when someone dies,
we tend to ask God "Why?"
I know I should not question him, but I do.

Oh death, what a terrible thing.
Is there a point to living if
we all are going to die?
We are living to die.

Why put me here if it ends in death?
I don't want to die, do I have a choice?
I can't live forever, no one can.

It is sad, we just have to live
the best life until the Lord sends
for us to come home to the Father.

O death, what a terrible thing.

Tsonya Hankerson
11th Grade

Death Be Toxic

Kelly has death in his pocket,
I might get it tattooed
Ya'll don't know my method's toxic.

Ya'll heard,
Slim coping options
so I keep it to myself
while so called friends are watching.

Ha…
Fake smile when I'm walking,
they don't know the façade is up,
few wonder why I ain't talking.

To the point,
I'm not alright, but I'll get by,
every low is such a high til
I can't end with a good night.

Atrell Johnson
12th Grade

I am Death

Generations past, present and future

the one who took your grandmother away
    and caused your mother grief,

the one who took your mother
    and cause you grief,

the one who will take you
    and cause your children grief,

the one who will take the children
    and cause their children to grief.

I am death

Generations past, present and future,

No one is immune to me,

I am for all eternity.

Naomi Alves
11th Grade

Self-Control

Self -control
control yourself

If you use self-control
it may improve your health.

If you are going through some stuff
self-control can help.

Self-control,
use it.

Khalil Vargas
8th Grade

Clown

You,
I like the way you think,
I probably just need a drink.

I thought I saw Lee,
down by the little tree.

I must look like a clown
I hope I don't make her frown.

When it is just you and me,
I think you deserve
a crown.

Dorly Beauplian
8th Grade

Count to 10

When you try to hurt someone,
and it gets out of hand,

If you are starting to get annoyed,
just count from 10.

If you want to calm down
instead of fighting people,

Just take a deep breath or
have a glass of water.

Put a smile on,
don't be grumpy,
play with friends,
I am not putting the jive on.

If you listen to me,
you will be happy,
count to 10,
you will feel better.

Samad Lamb
11th Grade

The authority
of those
who teach
is often
an obstacle
to those
who want
to learn.

-Marcus Tullius Cicero

Emotional Sobriety

The ability to
control oneself
is to not let
emotions get
out of hand.
When the ability
is lost
take care
of yourself.

The words
you say
may get
you banned
If you
have self-control
You can
improve
your reactions.

Abraham Merlin
12th Grade

Attitudes

Negative
Sometimes people
try to expose
what is wrong
with you
because they
cannot handle
what is
right with you.

Positive
Positive attitude
may not solve
all of your problems,
but it will
give you enough
strength and confidence
to overcome
problems on
your own.

Alana Syphus
6th Grade

Staying Strong

You have
to be strong,
whether
things go
right or wrong.

If you have
a strong will,
you will
reach your goals.

Sometimes being
the only strong one
can is tough,
since not many
will
wish
you luck.

Charlie Collins
11th Grade

Survival

so sad
so dreadful
makes me want
to cry and hide.

too much work,
too many people,
can I just burn it
with my anger or
drop out of this hell?

too much sadness
fills this classroom,
rude people all over the place.

Survive.
Survive.

don't try to learn,
  you'll forget it anyway.

Kamila Araujo
6th Grade

Best Part of Education

Pour on the lotion.
Rub it in,
perfect for my
summer skin.

On my bike,
or in the pool,
for me
there is
no more
school.

Joshua Torres
11ᵗʰ Grade

Exam

Now I lay me
down to rest,
I pray I pass
tomorrow's
college test.
Should I die
before I wake,
That's one
last test
I'll have
to take.

Tiffany Mkhizi
6th Grade

Investment

Going to College
may feel strange
but is an investment
in your intellect range.

You may not know
what is the next chapter,
but college will
make you as strong
as a velociraptor.

You will take a leap
into the fire and
come out a high flyer.

Remember to push through,
it will work for me,
and
it will work for you!

Jahell Paul
8th Grade

Stress

Stressing and stressing
about getting
assignments done,
hoping one day
I know what
is to become,
making friends
and memories
hoping they last, l
earning lessons
about life
I hope
to pass.

Ashanti Roario
11th Grade

Investment

College is stressing,
becoming a better person.

Too many classes,
not a lot of friends,
sleeping challenges ahead,
perhaps afternoon classes.

Out of the comfort zone;
academic successes
help the family.

John Hugo
12th Grade

A university cannot
make an imbecile
less of a fool,
neither can it make a warped
mind straight;
it is supposed to be a
laboratory for the inquisitive
mind
so he or she can take
advantage of its
academic resources.

-Lamine Pearlheart

How to Cook

Tingling your stomach
in cheer,

Thy food brings
different emotions as aftermath,

yet the satisfaction
will always be my habitat.

To learn how
satisfyingly cooking is thee,

Aroma sprints up
above the atmosphere.

Zezlet Depano
11th Grade

Wealth consists not in having
great possessions, but in
having few wants.

-Epictetus

While money cannot buy
happiness, it certainly lets
you choose your own form of
misery.

-Groucho Marx

Getting a Job

I have always
worked for my money,
the fresh stack
of dollar bills
smelling like honey.

I go to work
day by day
to have "my" money
to go out and play.

You have a chance
to take responsibility
for being an adult
adult "practice" for
        him or herself.

Shadira Herk
11th Grade

Funny Money

Money is
something.
We desire
buckets full
to comfortably
retire.

The value
of money through years
may change,
the currency markets
are strange.

We need money.
I want to buy a bunny.
Yea, that would be funny.
It would make
my life sunny.

Kuadir Johnson
8th Grade

Bricks

Not just
a new destination,
this is
the new horizon,
not just
a new role,
this is
the dream run.

Stack
the
money,
not the
funny.

Ronnie Stokes
12th Grade

Budgeting is Key

Have a
sweet home
the
American dream;
budgeting
is free
if
you want
a key chain
with
a
house key.

Jaeden Acosta
12th Grade

Credit Score

I want a new house
Bank says "No, your credit is too low"
Gen Z is so screwed.

Abigail Rooney
11th Grade

Filing Taxes

The dreaded time of the year;
the one that feels quite queer,
the season has arrived honey, to say
good-bye to hard earned money.

Fear not my dear friend,
and do not follow my trend,
file on time to keep what's yours, instead
of paying fines like household chores.

If you run out of time,
ask the I.R.S. for a filing extend,
if you rush and make mistakes,
you will file for a 1040X amend.

The I.R.S. will hold your hand through the
ordeal, the government is good
at giving free meals, unless you
want to be jailed for tax evasion.

There is little point in my persuasion,
pay our taxes on time, or the IRS will
cut you in your wage earning prime.

Andrew Heinzman
12th Grade

Horseless Carriage

loud & expensive
big & dangerous
make the earth dirty
Chevy
limousines
convertibles
no matter the kind or model
they suck
they mock
they slow my walk

Kamila Araujo
6th Grade

Cars

Whose car is that?
I think I know,
its's owner is quite happy though.
Full of joy like a vivid rainbow,
I watch him laugh, I cry hello.

He give his car a shake
and laughs until his belly aches.
The only other sound is the break of
distant waves and birds now awake.

The car is nice, shiny and clean.
He has promises and he has dreams.
After a dark afternoon with lots of rain,
He sleeps so he can avoid the pain.

John Meza
12th Grade

Some beautiful paths
can't be discovered
without getting lost.

-*Erol Ozan*

Take it easy driving -
the life you may save
may be mine.

-*James Dean*

Anger

When I have
lost my temper,
and my reason too.
I am never proud
of anything
I angerly do.

When I have
talked in anger
My cheeks flamed in read
I have always uttered
Something I wish
I had not said.

In anger I have
done deeds
not acting wise,
In anger I end up
having to apologize.

Looking back
across my life and
all I have lost or made,
I cannot recall
a single time
when my fury
ever paid.

Kayla Sandomenico
11th Grade

Depression

All my feelings stay compressed with the thoughts I process. Darkness is what I seek, hoping it will fell all   the creeks. I begin to fall in my self-made walls. My screaming demons have become my best friends.

All these false smiles, I hide behind the truth, feeling all the voices in my head, knowing one day it will lead   to my death. I am tired of life, I am tired of the fight, I   just want to give up, it is my right.

All the battles I face, have left marks and scrapes, all   the restless night when all I do is cry, are the nights I   want to die. All these scars shining through, no one   helps and I feel like the fool. Little do they know, all I   crave is a simple, "Are you okay?"

All these tears screaming down my face, showing my disgrace, feelings of guilt and displeasure, but how can I so sure?

Anonymous
12th Grade

Perseverance

Life can be depressing
many choose to use dope
just stay positive and
overcome your fear with hope.

Life can be stressful
all you need is motivation
just sharpen the saw and
you will feel the difference

Life can be difficult
but problems are not permanent
keep your nose to the grindstone
and achieve your goals.

Life can be cruel
just stay calm
just be patient and
wait your turn.

Filza Latiff
12th Grade

The best and most
beautiful things in the
world cannot be seen or
touched. They must be felt
with the heart.

-Helen Keller

One thing you can't hide –
is when you're crippled on
the inside.

-John Lennon

Social Media

What is true beauty today?

Does it mean getting 700 plus "likes?"

Does it mean putting on
    two pounds of makeup?

That is such an ugly picture,
why would she upload that picture?

Why is it photoshopped?

Why does she stand like that?

She is so fat,
    why did she not use a filter?

Shemar Beaucluch
12th Grade

Black Air Force

Black Air Force activities
I know the ways,
I am not a barber,
I don't do fades.

Black Air Force activity here,
Black Air Force activity there,
Black Air Force activity everywhere.

I do this all the time
with complete anonymity,
for I am the best at
Black Air Force activities

Bryan Sierra
11th Grade

Note: B.A.F. is code for criminal activity.

Christmas

In summertime
my branches were a place
for the birds to nest.

In autumn
my branches were
their place to rest,

Now that wintertime is here,
I hope to be all glistening,
bright with snowflakes…

The little birds Christmas tree!

Vanessa Roman
6th Grade

Babies

too fat,
too small,
so loud and unproductive.
they cry, cry, cry and
cry and cry.
they eat too much
so I'll eat them.
babies suck
and the only ones
that can stay
are plastic.

Kamila Araujo
6th Grade

Mom

My mother goes through many battles. She is the
shepherd and I am the cattle.

We pray to God each morning and thank him for
everything, to experience what it would be
like to not have anything.

I am grateful that she pushes me harder, to only
make sure I do not fall to the bottom.

Friends always ask me who is my role model, I
say my mother because no one can top her.

The only people who looked out for Mom were
God and Grandma, from heaven, her friends
and family praise her.

My mother always stays positive when times are
down, that's why I do my best to not let her
down.

Christian Thomas-Spletzer
8th Grade

Gun Violence

I walked down the aisle
of the corner store
Little did I know
I would be alive no more.
Coming quickly I heard
the monsters' feet,
Little did I know I
my spirit would be
getting its final blow.

Quicker and quicker
he came by,
In my stupor
I let out a sigh.
He ran down the aisle
And I ran fast
in the limited space,
He ran, at a faster pace.

He walked around the corner,
We squared face to face.
A gun pointed at me and
And I am no more.
It was the end of my time and
Also the end of this sad rhyme.

Phoenix Gonzalez
6th Grade

Angelic Rain of Bullets

To be born in a safe environment
To raise a child is harder to do
Going to school as normal life
One day the child is bullied.

The father the family leaves
The mother with troubles breathes
The child falls into depress
Wants to end it in suicide.

The bullied thinks of the bullies and
Goes to school with his MP5,
Brings enough ammo to kill one hundred ten.
He shoots his bullies and
Accidentally a friend.

Painted red are the floors,
the police crash the doors
"Robert!" the police call and with shots fired
Falls on the floor into concusity.

He goes to court with mother,
Five years sent away by the jury.
The next day his mother dies of asthma,
    That night the bullied is found dead
By self-infliction with knife in hand.

Miguel Alvelo-Torres
11th Grade

Jungle Warfare

Walking through high grass fields
With hope and life
A weapon to wield
In a place remote.

The family is sad
Which deepens with time
Death is your Dad
Time to meet the Grim Reaper.

Explosion sound far away
Living in hell
Where violence is the way
I am trapped in this jungle cell.

This war is hot
For freedom and country
Was the battle cry of this fight
Now I think about death every night.

Jungle theater warfare is a mess,
I live in the heart of darkness.

Anonymous

METS Charter Shutting Down

Dickenson is where I wanted to play,
Mom said METS is where I will stay.

So I got mad and prayed,
that the school would get washed away.

METS was caught off guard by the state
and failed to keep trouble away.

The school is currently in struggle and pain,
as it slowly swirls down the drain.

Next year I will be happy as ever,
going for lunch and enjoying the weather.

As the teachers scurry for jobs, the walls
and ceilings of 211 Sherman Ave will rot.

I shall walk out the last day with joyful laugh,
my dream of going to Dickenson is true at last.

Anonymous

METS is Closing

Oh no, my school is closing!
Next year, here am I going?
Where are you going?
Students are lurching and searching.

Should I go here
or there,
or anywhere?

The end is coming;
The end is coming…
The end is here,
Snyder I will go.

Wishing and hoping for the best.
Where I go is the mess
where I must rest.

Annonymous
8th Grade

Smoke Breaks and Candy Crush

In 2018,
research showed
that workers
who take smoke breaks
during work
waste 6 days
of productivity
a year.

Research also shows.
workers lose 8 hours
a week of productivity
by playing
on their cell phones
equaling 10 days
of productivity
a year.

Non-smokers
are asking
for an extra
six days of
vacation per year.

I should get
an extra 16 days
of vacation since
I neither smoke
nor own
a cell phone.

Gumby & Mr. Roboto
Circa 1990

My former college dorm neighbor becomes a teacher
in Vermont. His name was Peter, we called him
"Gumby," and his students called him Mr. W. Gumby
is creative, humorous history teacher with his smart
aleck Long Island attitude and love for God and the
heart of a servant.

On this Spring day he teaches a lesson about robots on
the playground and asks for a volunteer that he wraps
in aluminum foil and masking tape while playing the
song "Mr. Roboto" by the rock group Styx.

Sammy volunteers and happens to suffer from
albinism. Sammy walks around in a robotic suit
of aluminum foil on this hot day, reflecting off his
robotic suit, as Mr. W. teaches his lesson to the
background music of "Mr. Roboto."

Frantically, Sammy in a non-robotic voice screams,
"Mr. W, Mr. W, I am burning up! Help!. Help!
I am on fire!" The kid who was whiter than white, was
cooking faster than the song "Hot, Hot, Hot!" by
Buster Poindexter. Several kids jumped in ripping the
aluminum foil off Sammy like a Christmas gift
whose body looked like a New Years Day Ham.

When turning a human into a robot on a warm sunny
day, it is best to avoid using students surviving from
albinism.

Teacher's Lunch Room
West Milford High School
November 2018

Blah, blah, blah…
Does anyone watch the
Naked and Afraid TV Show?

Yea – blah, blah, blah.

Imagine trying
to survive 21 days
in the jungle naked
with all those wild
animals and insects.

I chime in,

Working in a
public school is
like being on the show
Naked and Afraid,
but
without the
naked part.

The teachers laugh
and nod in agreement as they
chew, chomp on their dinner
leftovers of meatloaf, pizza and
baked chicken legs the day
before the Thanksgiving break.

Confession 62

Fire Drills

As a teacher
when I had
no students
in class,
I hid
in my room
at least
4-5 times
during the
monthly
fire drill;

I was
working
on
school work
or
the weather
was
cold
or
inclement.

Jersey City Lockdown 12/10/2020

I begin working at METs Charter School – Jersey City Campus – in mid-September of 2019.

My commute to work is one hour but two hours home in bumper to bumper traffic. In the morning I drive around looking for a parking spot with alternative street parking. I witness stray cats, raccoons, and skunks walking the streets of a city next to the Hudson River across from the Manhattan skyline.

As I stroll to school, I pass the corner where two workers sitting in their van smoke their daily chronic jay bone. While I do not partake, I enjoy the smell.

I pass joggers, the corner bodega, the home with glazed green clay pots on the stairwell, the Jeep with the "Wander Forever" sticker on the back window and the white cat who greets me two to three times a week when I say, "Good morning puss, puss."

On the morning of clear skies and a full moon, our school will have a "Lock Down" announced at 2:30pm.

Since the Columbine High School Shooting in 1999, part of the monthly school schedules have been practicing "Lock Downs," where doors are locked, and no one is allowed out of the classroom or into the schools until the "all clear" has been announced.

The practice drills usually last 3-4 minutes, but on January 10th of 2019, no "all clea"r is announced.

Students begin getting antsy at 2:55pm, since dismissal takes place at 2:57pm. The "all clear is not announced at 2:57pm, or 3:30pm, or 4pm, and students want to leave. I go on the computer and see the school has posted the following warning: "The Jersey City police calling for a lockdown of all Jersey City schools until further notice."

By 5:30pm, the internet has articles posted by all the local television stations that there has been a gun fight for several hours in downtown Jersey City. At 5:55pm, it is announced one police officer, two store owners a store customer and the shooter couple have been shot and killed.

The killers turn out to be Black Hebrews who do not like Hebrews who are not Black Hebrews;   it is deemed a "hate crime."

The class becomes quiet after learning the news. At 6pm, the students are dismissed.

Not all lockdowns are for practice. I think, if this had to happen, I wish it had been on a Professional Development Day, because those meetings are
B-O-R-I-N-G.

Sinus Headache
January 2020

3 am: splitting sinus headache

3:01 am: a few curse words

3:04 am: Sudafed – watch Forensic Files on TV

3:20 am: left side of head beginning to clear

3:21 am: Vicks Vapor Rub on chest and nostrils

4:29 am: take "breathe-easy" strip off the nose

4:30 am: hot shower

4:35 am: left side of head 90% cleared

4:40 am: cough drops

5 am: right side of head still hurting

5:30 am: leave for work on this 16 degree day

5:45 am   take two Excedrin pills

6 am: most of congestion gone

6:45 am: Ahhhhhh - RELIEF!

6:46 am: Amen, Hallelujah!

Confession 63
<u>Jersey City Day Laborers
circa the winter of 2019</u>

Twice a month during
the work day,
I treat myself to a
$1 McDonald's coffee
and Egg McMuffin.

When Micky D's
runs the
$1 special for a
second sandwich

I buy one
and give it to
the homeless guy
on the corner or one
of the undocumented
day laborers standing
by the mall entryway.

It is it part
of my tithe and
the pay off
is the grateful
smile on s
human mug.

The Committed Teacher

The High School teacher, aged 72, confided in me,
"I will be working until I am 76."

"Wow, you must really be committed to your craft!"

The septuagenarian pedagogue replied,
"I emigrated to this country late in my life.
I must work until age 76 to get my
Social Security 40 quarters (10 years) to
be eligible for Social Security and Medicare.

His commitment was to
getting healthcare and
retirement income was
equal to investing in
the future of teens.

I identify!

When I turn 65,
I plan on collecting
Social Security and
Medicare.
50% of the people I know
who have died,
before age 65!

Being a pensioner is not
for wussies or those who
are not able to live past age 65.

Newark Teachers Union Letter

February 5, 2020

Dear N.T.U. President,

Based on the articles I read in the morning papers, the Newark Teachers Union supported the Newark School Superintendent's proposal of closing four charter schools in Newark. I understand why public schools and unions would be against charter schools with no union affiliation.

Any argument that is controversial, is controversial because it has good arguments on both sides. I work at, METS Charter School (Jersey City Campus), <u>that does have union representation</u> via the ***New Jersey Education Association.***

<u>Unions are part of the solution of improving charter schools.</u> **Solidarity means showing support for your fellow union brother and sisters, especially in the pedagogical field.**

The next time you choose to close down a charter school in Newark, the union should focus on the schools without union representation. *This is not Solidarity! This is throwing your fellow union brothers and sisters under the bus. It is called "eating your own."*

When a union lose one member, it loses power. I am sorely disappointed and betrayed by the leadership of the Newark Teachers Union.

Jim Geist

Jim Geist

Mets Charter School   cc: NJEA President

Confession 65
Student Fight

As a
student fight
broke out
in the hallway
between
periods 3-4,
a petite
English teacher
with blond hair
hit me in the arm
and screeched,
"Get in there!
Break it up!"

I looked
at her and
wanted to say,

Sister,
in the age of
equal rights,
be my guest.
Step into the middle
of the crazed
student frenzy
and earn your
equal pay!

The Innocents in Jail

Research
Shows
4%
of the
incarcerated
are
innocent.

That
comes
to 90,000
wrongly
imprisoned
Americans.
The
Shawshank
Redemption
Movie
is
the
scariest
horror
movie
to
me.

Corey Wise of the Central Park Five circa 1989

1,2,3,4,5,6,7,8,9,10,11,12,13,14,15,16,17,18,19,20,21,22,23,24,
25,26,27,28,29,30,31,32,33,34,35,36,37,38,39,40,41,42,43,44,
45,46,47,48,49,50,51,52,53,54,55,56,57,58,59,60,61,62,63,64,
65,66,67,68,69,70,71,72,73,74,75,76,77,78,79,80,81,82,83,84
,85,86,87,88,89,90,91,92,93,94,95,95,96,97,98,99,100,101,102,
103,104,105,106,107,108,109,110,111,112,113,114,115,116,
117,118,119,120,121,122,123,124,125,126,127,128,129,130,
131,132,133,134,135,136,137,138,139,140,141,142,143,144,
145,146,147,148,149,150,151,152,153,154,155,156,157,158,
159,160,161,162,163,164,165,166,167,168,169,170,171,172,
173,174,175,176,177,178,179,180,181,182,183,184,185,186,
187,188,189,190,191,192,193,194,195,196,197,198,199,200,
201,202,203,204,205,206,207,208,209,210,211,212,213,214,
215,216,217,218,219,220,221,222,223,224,225,226,227,228,
229,230,231,232,233,234,235,236,237,238,239,240,241,242,
243,244,245,246,247,248,249,250,251,252,253,254,255,256,
257,258,259,260,261,262,263,264,265,266,267,268,269,270,
271,272,273,274,275,276,277,278,279,280,281,282,283,284,
285,286,287,288,289,290,291,292,293,294,295,296,297,298,
299,300,301,302,303,304,305,306,307,308,309,310,311,312,
313,314,315,316,317,318,319,320,321,322,323,324,325,326,
327,328,329,330,331,332,333,334,335,336,337,338,339,340,
341,342,343,344,345,346,347,348,349,350,351,252,353,354,
355,356,357,358,359,360,361,362,363,364,365…

1,2,3,4,5,6,7,8,9,10,11,12,13,14,15,16,17,18,19,20,21,22,23,24,
25,26,27,28,29,30,31,32,33,34,35,36,37,38,39,40,41,42,43,44,
45,46,47,48,49,50,51,52,53,54,55,56,57,58,59,60,61,62,63,64,
65,66,67,68,69,70,71,72,73,74,75,76,77,78,79,80,81,82,83,84
,85,86,87,88,89,90,91,92,93,94,95,95,96,97,98,99,100,101,102,
103,104,105,106,107,108,109,110,111,112,113,114,115,116,
117,118,119,120,121,122,123,124,125,126,127,128,129,130,

131,132,133,134,135,136,137,138,139,140,141,142,143,144,
145,146,147,148,149,150,151,152,153,154,155,156,157,158,
159,160,161,162,163,164,165,166,167,168,169,170,171,172,
173,174,175,176,177,178,179,180,181,182,183,184,185,186,
187,188,189,190,191,192,193,194,195,196,197,198,199,200,
201,202,203,204,205,206,207,208,209,210,211,212,213,214,
215,216,217,218,219,220,221,222,223,224,225,226,227,228,
229,230,231,232,233,234,235,236,237,238,239,240,241,242,
243,244,245,246,247,248,249,250,251,252,253,254,255,256,
257,258,259,260,261,262,263,264,265,266,267,268,269,270,
271,272,273,274,275,276,277,278,279,280,281,282,283,284,
285,286,287,288,289,290,291,292,293,294,295,296,297,298,
299,300,301,302,303,304,305,306,307,308,309,310,311,312,
313,314,315,316,317,318,319,320,321,322,323,324,325,326,
327,328,329,330,331,332,333,334,335,336,337,338,339,340,
341,342,343,344,345,346,347,348,349,350,351,252,353,354,
355,356,357,358,359,360,361,362,363,364,365…

1,2,3,4,5,6,7,8,9,10,11,12,13,14,15,16,17,18,19,20,21,22,23,24,
25,26,27,28,29,30,31,32,33,34,35,36,37,38,39,40,41,42,43,44,
45,46,47,48,49,50,51,52,53,54,55,56,57,58,59,60,61,62,63,64,
65,66,67,68,69,70,71,72,73,74,75,76,77,78,79,80,81,82,83,84
,85,86,87,88,89,90,91,92,93,94,95,95,96,97,98,99,100,101,102,
103,104,105,106,107,108,109,110,111,112,113,114,115,116,
117,118,119,120,121,122,123,124,125,126,127,128,129,130,
131,132,133,134,135,136,137,138,139,140,141,142,143,144,
145,146,147,148,149,150,151,152,153,154,155,156,157,158,
159,160,161,162,163,164,165,166,167,168,169,170,171,172,
173,174,175,176,177,178,179,180,181,182,183,184,185,186,
187,188,189,190,191,192,193,194,195,196,197,198,199,200,
201,202,203,204,205,206,207,208,209,210,211,212,213,214,
215,216,217,218,219,220,221,222,223,224,225,226,227,228,
229,230,231,232,233,234,235,236,237,238,239,240,241,242,
243,244,245,246,247,248,249,250,251,252,253,254,255,256,

257,258,259,260,261,262,263,264,265,266,267,268,269,270,
271,272,273,274,275,276,277,278,279,280,281,282,283,284,
285,286,287,288,289,290,291,292,293,294,295,296,297,298,
299,300,301,302,303,304,305,306,307,308,309,310,311,312,
313,314,315,316,317,318,319,320,321,322,323,324,325,326,
327,328,329,330,331,332,333,334,335,336,337,338,339,340,
341,342,343,344,345,346,347,348,349,350,351,252,353,354,
355,356,357,358,359,360,361,362,363,364,365…

1,2,3,4,5,6,7,8,9,10,11,12,13,14,15,16,17,18,19,20,21,22,23,24,
25,26,27,28,29,30,31,32,33,34,35,36,37,38,39,40,41,42,43,44,
45,46,47,48,49,50,51,52,53,54,55,56,57,58,59,60,61,62,63,64,
65,66,67,68,69,70,71,72,73,74,75,76,77,78,79,80,81,82,83,84
,85,86,87,88,89,90,91,92,93,94,95,95,96,97,98,99,100,101,102,
103,104,105,106,107,108,109,110,111,112,113,114,115,116,
117,118,119,120,121,122,123,124,125,126,127,128,129,130,
131,132,133,134,135,136,137,138,139,140,141,142,143,144,
145,146,147,148,149,150,151,152,153,154,155,156,157,158,
159,160,161,162,163,164,165,166,167,168,169,170,171,172,
173,174,175,176,177,178,179,180,181,182,183,184,185,186,
187,188,189,190,191,192,193,194,195,196,197,198,199,200,
201,202,203,204,205,206,207,208,209,210,211,212,213,214,
215,216,217,218,219,220,221,222,223,224,225,226,227,228,
229,230,231,232,233,234,235,236,237,238,239,240,241,242,
243,244,245,246,247,248,249,250,251,252,253,254,255,256,
257,258,259,260,261,262,263,264,265,266,267,268,269,270,
271,272,273,274,275,276,277,278,279,280,281,282,283,284,
285,286,287,288,289,290,291,292,293,294,295,296,297,298,
299,300,301,302,303,304,305,306,307,308,309,310,311,312,
313,314,315,316,317,318,319,320,321,322,323,324,325,326,
327,328,329,330,331,332,333,334,335,336,337,338,339,340,
341,342,343,344,345,346,347,348,349,350,351,252,353,354,
355,356,357,358,359,360,361,362,363,364,365…

1,2,3,4,5,6,7,8,9,10,11,12,13,14,15,16,17,18,19,20,21,22,23,24,

25,26,27,28,29,30,31,32,33,34,35,36,37,38,39,40,41,42,43,44,
45,46,47,48,49,50,51,52,53,54,55,56,57,58,59,60,61,62,63,64,
65,66,67,68,69,70,71,72,73,74,75,76,77,78,79,80,81,82,83,84
,85,86,87,88,89,90,91,92,93,94,95,95,96,97,98,99,100,101,102,
103,104,105,106,107,108,109,110,111,112,113,114,115,116,
117,118,119,120,121,122,123,124,125,126,127,128,129,130,
131,132,133,134,135,136,137,138,139,140,141,142,143,144,
145,146,147,148,149,150,151,152,153,154,155,156,157,158,
159,160,161,162,163,164,165,166,167,168,169,170,171,172,
173,174,175,176,177,178,179,180,181,182,183,184,185,186,
187,188,189,190,191,192,193,194,195,196,197,198,199,200,
201,202,203,204,205,206,207,208,209,210,211,212,213,214,
215,216,217,218,219,220,221,222,223,224,225,226,227,228,
229,230,231,232,233,234,235,236,237,238,239,240,241,242,
243,244,245,246,247,248,249,250,251,252,253,254,255,256,
257,258,259,260,261,262,263,264,265,266,267,268,269,270,
271,272,273,274,275,276,277,278,279,280,281,282,283,284,
285,286,287,288,289,290,291,292,293,294,295,296,297,298,
299,300,301,302,303,304,305,306,307,308,309,310,311,312,
313,314,315,316,317,318,319,320,321,322,323,324,325,326,
327,328,329,330,331,332,333,334,335,336,337,338,339,340,
341,342,343,344,345,346,347,348,349,350,351,252,353,354,
355,356,357,358,359,360,361,362,363,364,365…

1,2,3,4,5,6,7,8,9,10,11,12,13,14,15,16,17,18,19,20,21,22,23,24,
25,26,27,28,29,30,31,32,33,34,35,36,37,38,39,40,41,42,43,44,
45,46,47,48,49,50,51,52,53,54,55,56,57,58,59,60,61,62,63,64,
65,66,67,68,69,70,71,72,73,74,75,76,77,78,79,80,81,82,83,84
,85,86,87,88,89,90,91,92,93,94,95,95,96,97,98,99,100,101,102,
103,104,105,106,107,108,109,110,111,112,113,114,115,116,
117,118,119,120,121,122,123,124,125,126,127,128,129,130,
131,132,133,134,135,136,137,138,139,140,141,142,143,144,
145,146,147,148,149,150,151,152,153,154,155,156,157,158,
159,160,161,162,163,164,165,166,167,168,169,170,171,172,

173,174,175,176,177,178,179,180,181,182,183,184,185,186,
187,188,189,190,191,192,193,194,195,196,197,198,199,200,
201,202,203,204,205,206,207,208,209,210,211,212,213,214,
215,216,217,218,219,220,221,222,223,224,225,226,227,228,
229,230,231,232,233,234,235,236,237,238,239,240,241,242,
243,244,245,246,247,248,249,250,251,252,253,254,255,256,
257,258,259,260,261,262,263,264,265,266,267,268,269,270,
271,272,273,274,275,276,277,278,279,280,281,282,283,284,
285,286,287,288,289,290,291,292,293,294,295,296,297,298,
299,300,301,302,303,304,305,306,307,308,309,310,311,312,
313,314,315,316,317,318,319,320,321,322,323,324,325,326,
327,328,329,330,331,332,333,334,335,336,337,338,339,340,
341,342,343,344,345,346,347,348,349,350,351,252,353,354,
355,356,357,358,359,360,361,362,363,364,365…

1,2,3,4,5,6,7,8,9,10,11,12,13,14,15,16,17,18,19,20,21,22,23,24,
25,26,27,28,29,30,31,32,33,34,35,36,37,38,39,40,41,42,43,44,
45,46,47,48,49,50,51,52,53,54,55,56,57,58,59,60,61,62,63,64,
65,66,67,68,69,70,71,72,73,74,75,76,77,78,79,80,81,82,83,84
,85,86,87,88,89,90,91,92,93,94,95,95,96,97,98,99,100,101,102,
103,104,105,106,107,108,109,110,111,112,113,114,115,116,
117,118,119,120,121,122,123,124,125,126,127,128,129,130,
131,132,133,134,135,136,137,138,139,140,141,142,143,144,
145,146,147,148,149,150,151,152,153,154,155,156,157,158,
159,160,161,162,163,164,165,166,167,168,169,170,171,172,
173,174,175,176,177,178,179,180,181,182,183,184,185,186,
187,188,189,190,191,192,193,194,195,196,197,198,199,200,
201,202,203,204,205,206,207,208,209,210,211,212,213,214,
215,216,217,218,219,220,221,222,223,224,225,226,227,228,
229,230,231,232,233,234,235,236,237,238,239,240,241,242,
243,244,245,246,247,248,249,250,251,252,253,254,255,256,
257,258,259,260,261,262,263,264,265,266,267,268,269,270,
271,272,273,274,275,276,277,278,279,280,281,282,283,284,
285,286,287,288,289,290,291,292,293,294,295,296,297,298,

299,300,301,302,303,304,305,306,307,308,309,310,311,312,
313,314,315,316,317,318,319,320,321,322,323,324,325,326,
327,328,329,330,331,332,333,334,335,336,337,338,339,340,
341,342,343,344,345,346,347,348,349,350,351,252,353,354,
355,356,357,358,359,360,361,362,363,364,365…

1,2,3,4,5,6,7,8,9,10,11,12,13,14,15,16,17,18,19,20,21,22,23,24,
25,26,27,28,29,30,31,32,33,34,35,36,37,38,39,40,41,42,43,44,
45,46,47,48,49,50,51,52,53,54,55,56,57,58,59,60,61,62,63,64,
65,66,67,68,69,70,71,72,73,74,75,76,77,78,79,80,81,82,83,84
,85,86,87,88,89,90,91,92,93,94,95,95,96,97,98,99,100,101,102,
103,104,105,106,107,108,109,110,111,112,113,114,115,116,
117,118,119,120,121,122,123,124,125,126,127,128,129,130,
131,132,133,134,135,136,137,138,139,140,141,142,143,144,
145,146,147,148,149,150,151,152,153,154,155,156,157,158,
159,160,161,162,163,164,165,166,167,168,169,170,171,172,
173,174,175,176,177,178,179,180,181,182,183,184,185,186,
187,188,189,190,191,192,193,194,195,196,197,198,199,200,
201,202,203,204,205,206,207,208,209,210,211,212,213,214,
215,216,217,218,219,220,221,222,223,224,225,226,227,228,
229,230,231,232,233,234,235,236,237,238,239,240,241,242,
243,244,245,246,247,248,249,250,251,252,253,254,255,256,
257,258,259,260,261,262,263,264,265,266,267,268,269,270,
271,272,273,274,275,276,277,278,279,280,281,282,283,284,
285,286,287,288,289,290,291,292,293,294,295,296,297,298,
299,300,301,302,303,304,305,306,307,308,309,310,311,312,
313,314,315,316,317,318,319,320,321,322,323,324,325,326,
327,328,329,330,331,332,333,334,335,336,337,338,339,340,
341,342,343,344,345,346,347,348,349,350,351,252,353,354,
355,356,357,358,359,360,361,362,363,364,365…

1,2,3,4,5,6,7,8,9,10,11,12,13,14,15,16,17,18,19,20,21,22,23,24,
25,26,27,28,29,30,31,32,33,34,35,36,37,38,39,40,41,42,43,44,
45,46,47,48,49,50,51,52,53,54,55,56,57,58,59,60,61,62,63,64,

65,66,67,68,69,70,71,72,73,74,75,76,77,78,79,80,81,82,83,84
,85,86,87,88,89,90,91,92,93,94,95,95,96,97,98,99,100,101,102,
103,104,105,106,107,108,109,110,111,112,113,114,115,116,
117,118,119,120,121,122,123,124,125,126,127,128,129,130,
131,132,133,134,135,136,137,138,139,140,141,142,143,144,
145,146,147,148,149,150,151,152,153,154,155,156,157,158,
159,160,161,162,163,164,165,166,167,168,169,170,171,172,
173,174,175,176,177,178,179,180,181,182,183,184,185,186,
187,188,189,190,191,192,193,194,195,196,197,198,199,200,
201,202,203,204,205,206,207,208,209,210,211,212,213,214,
215,216,217,218,219,220,221,222,223,224,225,226,227,228,
229,230,231,232,233,234,235,236,237,238,239,240,241,242,
243,244,245,246,247,248,249,250,251,252,253,254,255,256,
257,258,259,260,261,262,263,264,265,266,267,268,269,270,
271,272,273,274,275,276,277,278,279,280,281,282,283,284,
285,286,287,288,289,290,291,292,293,294,295,296,297,298,
299,300,301,302,303,304,305,306,307,308,309,310,311,312,
313,314,315,316,317,318,319,320,321,322,323,324,325,326,
327,328,329,330,331,332,333,334,335,336,337,338,339,340,
341,342,343,344,345,346,347,348,349,350,351,252,353,354,
355,356,357,358,359,360,361,362,363,364,365…

1,2,3,4,5,6,7,8,9,10,11,12,13,14,15,16,17,18,19,20,21,22,23,24,
25,26,27,28,29,30,31,32,33,34,35,36,37,38,39,40,41,42,43,44,
45,46,47,48,49,50,51,52,53,54,55,56,57,58,59,60,61,62,63,64,
65,66,67,68,69,70,71,72,73,74,75,76,77,78,79,80,81,82,83,84
,85,86,87,88,89,90,91,92,93,94,95,95,96,97,98,99,100,101,102,
103,104,105,106,107,108,109,110,111,112,113,114,115,116,
117,118,119,120,121,122,123,124,125,126,127,128,129,130,
131,132,133,134,135,136,137,138,139,140,141,142,143,144,
145,146,147,148,149,150,151,152,153,154,155,156,157,158,
159,160,161,162,163,164,165,166,167,168,169,170,171,172,
173,174,175,176,177,178,179,180,181,182,183,184,185,186,
187,188,189,190,191,192,193,194,195,196,197,198,199,200,

201,202,203,204,205,206,207,208,209,210,211,212,213,214,
215,216,217,218,219,220,221,222,223,224,225,226,227,228,
229,230,231,232,233,234,235,236,237,238,239,240,241,242,
243,244,245,246,247,248,249,250,251,252,253,254,255,256,
257,258,259,260,261,262,263,264,265,266,267,268,269,270,
271,272,273,274,275,276,277,278,279,280,281,282,283,284,
285,286,287,288,289,290,291,292,293,294,295,296,297,298,
299,300,301,302,303,304,305,306,307,308,309,310,311,312,
313,314,315,316,317,318,319,320,321,322,323,324,325,326,
327,328,329,330,331,332,333,334,335,336,337,338,339,340,
341,342,343,344,345,346,347,348,349,350,351,252,353,354,
355,356,357,358,359,360,361,362,363,364,365…

1,2,3,4,5,6,7,8,9,10,11,12,13,14,15,16,17,18,19,20,21,22,23,24,
25,26,27,28,29,30,31,32,33,34,35,36,37,38,39,40,41,42,43,44,
45,46,47,48,49,50,51,52,53,54,55,56,57,58,59,60,61,62,63,64,
65,66,67,68,69,70,71,72,73,74,75,76,77,78,79,80,81,82,83,84
,85,86,87,88,89,90,91,92,93,94,95,95,96,97,98,99,100,101,102,
103,104,105,106,107,108,109,110,111,112,113,114,115,116,
117,118,119,120,121,122,123,124,125,126,127,128,129,130,
131,132,133,134,135,136,137,138,139,140,141,142,143,144,
145,146,147,148,149,150,151,152,153,154,155,156,157,158,
159,160,161,162,163,164,165,166,167,168,169,170,171,172,
173,174,175,176,177,178,179,180,181,182,183,184,185,186,
187,188,189,190,191,192,193,194,195,196,197,198,199,200,
201,202,203,204,205,206,207,208,209,210,211,212,213,214,
215,216,217,218,219,220,221,222,223,224,225,226,227,228,
229,230,231,232,233,234,235,236,237,238,239,240,241,242,
243,244,245,246,247,248,249,250,251,252,253,254,255,256,
257,258,259,260,261,262,263,264,265,266,267,268,269,270,
271,272,273,274,275,276,277,278,279,280,281,282,283,284,
285,286,287,288,289,290,291,292,293,294,295,296,297,298,
299,300,301,302,303,304,305,306,307,308,309,310,311,312,
313,314,315,316,317,318,319,320,321,322,323,324,325,326,

327,328,329,330,331,332,333,334,335,336,337,338,339,340,
341,342,343,344,345,346,347,348,349,350,351,252,353,354,
355,356,357,358,359,360,361,362,363,364,365…

1,2,3,4,5,6,7,8,9,10,11,12,13,14,15,16,17,18,19,20,21,22,23,24,
25,26,27,28,29,30,31,32,33,34,35,36,37,38,39,40,41,42,43,44,
45,46,47,48,49,50,51,52,53,54,55,56,57,58,59,60,61,62,63,64,
65,66,67,68,69,70,71,72,73,74,75,76,77,78,79,80,81,82,83,84
,85,86,87,88,89,90,91,92,93,94,95,95,96,97,98,99,100,101,102,
103,104,105,106,107,108,109,110,111,112,113,114,115,116,
117,118,119,120,121,122,123,124,125,126,127,128,129,130,
131,132,133,134,135,136,137,138,139,140,141,142,143,144,
145,146,147,148,149,150,151,152,153,154,155,156,157,158,
159,160,161,162,163,164,165,166,167,168,169,170,171,172,
173,174,175,176,177,178,179,180,181,182,183,184,185,186,
187,188,189,190,191,192,193,194,195,196,197,198,199,200,
201,202,203,204,205,206,207,208,209,210,211,212,213,214,
215,216,217,218,219,220,221,222,223,224,225,226,227,228,
229,230,231,232,233,234,235,236,237,238,239,240,241,242,
243,244,245,246,247,248,249,250,251,252,253,254,255,256,
257,258,259,260,261,262,263,264,265,266,267,268,269,270,
271,272,273,274,275,276,277,278,279,280,281,282,283,284,
285,286,287,288,289,290,291,292,293,294,295,296,297,298,
299,300,301,302,303,304,305,306,307,308,309,310,311,312,
313,314,315,316,317,318,319,320,321,322,323,324,325,326,
327,328,329,330,331,332,333,334,335,336,337,338,339,340,
341,342,343,344,345,346,347,348,349,350,351,252,353,354,
355,356,357,358,359,360,361,362,363,364,365…

1,2,3,4,5,6,7,8,9,10,11,12,13,14,15,16,17,18,19,20,21,22,23,24,
25,26,27,28,29,30,31,32,33,34,35,36,37,38,39,40,41,42,43,44,
45,46,47,48,49,50,51,52,53,54,55,56,57,58,59,60,61,62,63,64,
65,66,67,68,69,70,71,72,73,74,75,76,77,78,79,80,81,82,83,84
,85,86,87,88,89,90,91,92,93,94,95,95,96,97,98,99,100,101,102,

103,104,105,106,107,108,109,110,111,112,113,114,115,116,
117,118,119,120,121,122,123,124,125,126,127,128,129,130,
131,132,133,134,135,136,137,138,139,140,141,142,143,144,
145,146,147,148,149,150,151,152,153,154,155,156,157,158,
159,160,161,162,163,164,165,166,167,168,169,170,171,172,
173,174,175,176,177,178,179,180,181,182,183,184,185,186,
187,188,189,190,191,192,193,194,195,196,197,198,199,200,
201,202,203,204,205,206,207,208,209,210,211,212,213,214,
215,216,217,218,219,220,221,222,223,224,225,226,227,228,
229,230,231,232,233,234,235,236,237,238,239,240,241,242,
243,244,245,246,247,248,249,250,251,252,253,254,255,256,
257,258,259,260,261,262,263,264,265,266,267,268,269,270,
271,272,273,274,275,276,277,278,279,280,281,282,283,284,
285,286,287,288,289,290,291,292,293,294,295,296,297,298,
299,300,301,302,303,304,305,306,307,308,309,310,311,312,
313,314,315,316,317,318,319,320,321,322,323,324,325,326,
327,328,329,330,331,332,333,334,335,336,337,338,339,340,
341,342,343,344,345,346,347,348,349,350,351,252,353,354,
355,356,357,358,359,360,361,362,363,364,365…

1,2,3,4,5,6,7,8,9,10,11,12,13,14,15,16,17,18,19,20,21,22,23,24,
25,26,27,28,29,30,31,32,33,34,35,36,37,38,39,40,41,42,43,44,
45,46,47,48,49,50,51,52,53,54,55,56,57,58,59,60,61,62,63,64,
65,66,67,68,69,70,71,72,73,74,75,76,77,78,79,80,81,82,83,84
,85,86,87,88,89,90,91,92,93,94,95,95,96,97,98,99,100,101,102,
103,104,105,106,107,108,109,110,111,112,113,114,115,116,
117,118,119,120,121,122,123,124,125,126,127,128,129,130,
131,132,133,134,135,136,137,138,139,140,141,142,143,144,
145,146,147,148,149,150,151,152,153,154,155,156,157,158,
159,160,161,162,163,164,165,166,167,168,169,170,171,172,
173,174,175,176,177,178,179,180,181,182,183,184,185,186,
187,188,189,190,191,192,193,194,195,196,197,198,199,200,
201,202,203,204,205,206,207,208,209,210,211,212,213,214,
215,216,217,218,219,220,221,222,223,224,225,226,227,228,

229,230,231,232,233,234,235,236,237,238,239,240,241,242,
243,244,245,246,247,248,249,250,251,252,253,254,255,256,
257,258,259,260,261,262,263,264,265,266,267,268,269,270,
271,272,273,274,275,276,277,278,279,280,281,282,283,284,
285,286,287,288,289,290,291,292,293,294,295,296,297,298,
299,300,301,302,303,304,305,306,307,308,309,310,311,312,
313,314,315,316,317,318,319,320,321,322,323,324,325,326,
327,328,329,330,331,332,333,334,335,336,337,338,339,340,
341,342,343,344,345,346,347,348,349,350,351,252,353,354,
355,356,357,358,359,360,361,362,363,364,365…

1,2,3,4,5,6,7,8,9,10,11,12,13,14,15,16,17,18,19,20,21,22,23,24,
25,26,27,28,29,30,31,32,33,34,35,36,37,38,39,40,41,42,43,44,
45,46,47,48,49,50,51,52,53,54,55,56,57,58,59,60,61,62,63,64,
65,66,67,68,69,70,71,72,73,74,75,76,77,78,79,80,81,82,83,84
,85,86,87,88,89,90,91,92,93,94,95,95,96,97,98,99,100,101,102,
103,104,105,106,107,108,109,110,111,112,113,114,115,116,
117,118,119,120,121,122,123,124,125,126,127,128,129,130,
131,132,133,134,135,136,137,138,139,140,141,142,143,144,
145,146,147,148,149,150,151,152,153,154,155,156,157,158,
159,160,161,162,163,164,165,166,167,168,169,170,171,172,
173,174,175,176,177,178,179,180,181,182,183,184,185,186,
187,188,189,190,191,192,193,194,195,196,197,198,199,200,
201,202,203,204,205,206,207,208,209,210,211,212,213,214,
215,216,217,218,219,220,221,222,223,224,225,226,227,228,
229,230,231,232,233,234,235,236,237,238,239,240,241,242,
243,244,245,246,247,248,249,250,251,252,253,254,255,256,
257,258,259,260,261,262,263,264,265,266,267,268,269,270,
271,272,273,274,275,276,277,278,279,280,281,282,283,284,
285,286,287,288,289,290,291,292,293,294,295,296,297,298,
299,300,301,302,303,304,305,306,307,308,309,310,311,312,
313,314,315,316,317,318,319,320,321,322,323,324,325,326,
327,328,329,330,331,332,333,334,335,336,337,338,339,340,
341,342,343,344,345,346,347,348,349,350,351,252,353,354,
355,356,357,358,359,360,361,362,363,364,365…

The 5,110 days
of fourteen years
Corey Wise,
aged 16,
of the "The Central Park Five,"
spent in prison for
an alleged rape
in New York City,
that he
did not commit.

Diner Hipsters

The high school ladies
with purple hair were
escorted to their table
by the Diner Hostess.

The girls sad down,
looked at the menus and
then at their cell phones
before and after
placing their order with the waitress
and while they
consumed their lunch.

They looked at their cell phones
while they waited for their check
and only stopped looking at the cell phones
when they donned their jackets
and left a tip on the table.

As the Diner hipsters
exited the Diner,
one said to the other,
"Good talk!"

Zip-Zip-Zip

Attending Union Terrace Elementary
In the first half of the 1970's,
I am dancing to the song" One"
by Three Dog Night
at my 2nd grade Halloween celebration,

I could make my teacher Ms. Sotak laugh and laugh.
It felt good as a 7 year old to have some power
over an adult who graded my
math, language skills and classroom behavior
four times a year.

One day in the hallway on the way to the cafeteria,
I kept hearing this whisper of a sound
"zip, zip, zip, zip" as Ms. Sotak
escorted her 2nd grade class down to the cafeteria.
I could never figure out where the sound came from.

In 2019 as a teacher in my 19th year
as I walk down the hallway of METS Charter School
Jersey City Campus, I hear the
whisper of the "zip, zip, zip, zip."
I am brought back to the hallways of elementary school
boy days and REALIZE the whisper
is coming from between my thighs in my corduroy pants
rubbing against each other.

I will join Weight Watchers or become
the next victim of spontaneous combustion.